DATE DUE

Earthquake
Came to
Harlem

Earthquake Came to Harlem

Jackie Sheeler

The New York Quarterly Foundation, Inc.
New York, New York

NYQ Books™ is an imprint of The New York Quarterly Foundation, Inc.

The New York Quarterly Foundation, Inc.
P. O. Box 2015
Old Chelsea Station
New York, NY 10113

www.nyqbooks.org

First Edition

Set in Calibri

Layout and Design by Raymond P. Hammond

Cover layout and design by Kat Georges [katgeorges.com]

Library of Congress Control Number: 2010931335

ISBN: 978-1-935520-34-4

Earthquake Came to Harlem

ACKNOWLEDGMENTS

I'm grateful to the editors of the journals and anthologies in which versions of the following poems have appeared:

100 Poets Against the War (anthology): Collateral Damage
Comstock Review: Dream Me Coupled
Java Monkey Anthology: Infant Face of Desire (special thanks to Collin Kelley, who nominated this poem for a Pushcart Prize)
Long Island Sound Anthology: The Scissors of My Mother
Long Shot Magazine: Alien Periscopes; Turning Sweet 16 in Prison
New Millennium Writings: Pickup Line
New York Quarterly: Dad's Last Wife; Gloria's Stories; God Enters the World; The Maker
Ocho: Solo
Phoebe: Today Is the Day She Does It
Rattapallax: Cavepeople
Slant: Chrysanthemum
The Ledge: At the Office
The Lineup: Another Hallway Altar in the Projects; Anthony Baez
The Long Islander: In My Cell
Tribes: Playground of Face
Visions International: Interior Poured
Women of the Bowery Anthology: Marlboro Woman

The Memory Factory (Buttonwood Press, 2002): An Address I Could Never Find Again; One Uncivilized Soul; Red Tape; Shutting Down; The Memory Factory; To Xerox 3 Stapled Sheets

Heartfelt thanks to Ellen Bass for all the inspiration and guidance over the years; to Shelley Stenhouse for her wonderful editorial eye, and to Kat Georges—my partner in Pink Pony crime—for the magnificent cover design.

Special thanks to all my editors, past and present, for their support and generosity: David Radavich (Buttonwood Press); Daniel Nester (Soft Skull Press); Kat Georges (Three Rooms Press) and of course Raymond Hammond (NYQ Books), godfather of this collection.

How can you who are so holy suffer?
—A Course in Miracles

Melancholy is useful. Bring yours.
—Li-Young Li

Contents

The Maker

Diorama

Solo

My Enemy

The Maker

God Enters the World

God is shooting up again
disguised in heartbreak
and denim. He sits on a windowsill, one sleeve

rolled, arm
stiff as a plank, zeroed in
on tiny navigations.

He's forgotten his name. God
goes tricking in midtown, stoops
at car-windows, sashays

down sidestreets, rolls ten-dollar bills
into the lining of her shoplifted purse. God's into
costumes and amnesia, slips

entirely inside each fresh uniform,
leaves the heft of Godhood
out of all earthly reach.

God makes commercials
and blows herself to pieces in Jerusalem,
designs swimming pools and peddles Viagra

over the web. God enters the world godless—
unholy, powerless, blank: relinquishes
memory and might to become

consumed by the concerns of humanness
—but this you already know. How to live,
nameless, in the limits of a body

unable to recall what came before,
unable to agree on what comes after.

Underground Xmas

Out of the packed train comes a horizontal tree, pine
needles poking through tight

plastic wrap. She's wearing
a raincoat and a frown, the blue spruce

hugged in her strong arms like a Roman battering ram.
Commuters step aside, all sighs and clucks.

This woman loves someone enough
to bring them Christmas on the subway, wrestling

a tree twice her height through tongue-
sucking rush-hour crowds.

The sharp holiday scent of pine
enlivens the final car of the C train,

trails her to the 50th Street escalator
where she juggles the pungent

tree on her hip, ascending.

Collateral Damage

In a place of sand and wind, worn
cotton looped across her face,
a woman tends to her sons.

She owns no appliances, knows life
by the taste of cloth at her mouth.

Bread and leaflets drop from the sky,
then other things. Nothing hit the airport,
just half a mile north.

Street Doctorate

Russell lives in his wheelchair on my street.
Rain finds him underneath the nearby scaffold,
sucking on a crack pipe if he's had a lucky day.

One Saturday morning Russ spends hours on a three-
word sign, magic-marking each block letter:
HOMELESS—PELASE HELP

The skin on both his legs, his arms,
the back of his hands, side of his neck
is shiny, white with scar, not an unblemished

inch anywhere. I know what it takes
to create such specific disfigurations—to go
in, again and again, through

abscess and infection with the dull
tip of an overused needle,
holding your breath and gouging, until

fresh blood blooms in the barrel and it's safe
to squeeze off. Getting a hit
after the veins are gone is an art Russell has

mastered—his doctorate in self-destruction
earned in abandoned buildings, on rooftops, in alleys,
needlepointing his skin away

one pinprick at a time, patiently,
hour by hour by day,
until heroin has built him this new body

and brought him a pair of big steel wheels to sit between,
in rain and sun and streetlight,
under the temporary scaffold or beside the white

stone lions at the library, holding
his misspelled sign, pant-legs hiked to the knee,
bony ruins glowing in the light.

The Wager

If I place this empty grande Star-
Bucks cup carefully (i.e.: with

gentleness, precision) into
a half-full public trash bin

then maybe he will maybe
she will maybe they (some-
one) will come back—

if I smile at the wild-eyed
seat-snatching subway demon, wish

good day to the grim quarter-
counting crone at the corner laundry

then maybe he will maybe
she will maybe they (some-
one) will come back—

If I hold open doors for angry strangers
and skip over sidewalk cracks
if I never litter, always recycle, light a thousand
cinnamon candles and pretend to pray

then maybe this will maybe
it will maybe everything (my
life) will be okay

and maybe he will maybe
she will maybe they (some-
one) will stay—

Unknown, Grave #2

You, Unknown, are my special spreadsheet connection.
Nameless and sexless, I know two things about you
that I will never know about myself:
the date and the place of your death.

Seven years younger than I am today
you fell to the boardwalk planks and did not rise.
A stroke? A gunshot? An overdose?
The record book doesn't say.
Just a date without a time, a place without a reason.
Google tells me it was a Sunday, the weather
was fine. Nothing more. No paragraph about you
in the Daily News on 4/26/98.

I see a wrinkled jacket, denim legs
surrounded by a knot of blue police.
A silent ambulance rolling carefully
up the pedestrian ramp. I see medics
and a big zippered bag. Was it afternoon,
with all the chubby Russian sunbathers
watching them lift you into the white truck?
Were you a chubby Russian sunbather?
A long-muscled handball champion from the Brighton
Beach Courts? Flacco with a pocket full of magic dust?

Unknown, my young self walked that boardwalk
at least a thousand times. I didn't always carry ID.
I wasn't usually sober. Some nights
I slept beside a stranger on the bottlecap-dotted sand
or swam alone at midnight, my clothes
a tiny pile far behind me on the beach,
the blinking red light of the Parachute
my only guide. I always made it back.
I took making it back for granted.

Today Is the Day She Does It

...slides down the loop—

how perfectly
The woman hangs from her noose in the garden.

a bookmark for a blind man

brainskip...shush
Skates against childhood ice, such pirouettes.

scenes Scenes scenes repeat Repeat broken

stop stopped | here—
In the heart's narrow corridor.

Overtime

The Feldsteins have a colic baby:
he cries all night, can't eat, can't sleep

except in snatches—(Mrs. Feldstein breast-
feeds and the wheat she boils for breakfast

sickens her infant. But this is not the point.)
Baby dropped to sleep just ten minutes ago.

Mrs. F, pale with her all-day/all-night
walks and the incessant machinery of rocking,

sprawls on her brown velvet La-Z Boy,
goes out like a light. Her mouth, fallen

softly open, drools like her son's,
her closed eyes flicker, dreaming.

At the corner, a signal goes from red to green
and the lead driver, tired after weeks of double-shifting,

doesn't instantly hit the gas. Another driver
slams down his horn with both hands

and holds it, holds it, even as the cars
roll forward. Sally Feldstein falls

sideways out of her recliner—heart
hammering, eyes wide—stumbles

toward the nursery. Once again,
the baby has started to wail.

The Maker

God made AIDS, and gave it to himself in Greenwich
Village, while examining holy germhood
through the eyes of his microscope self.

God made the ocean to sit beside
on the night he was bereft, seeking
comfort in the rhythms of his largeness.

God made the Trade Center
because he needed a place to watch the city
over good food late at night with rich companions
and a place to aim his flaming planes.

God sits beside me on the brownstone stoop,
with one hand on my face, one hand on a trigger.
He pulls up my blanket and slams shut a cell.

His love is everywhere, bright as radium,
potent as a payload.

Meat Locker: An Equation

Unfortunate math: 5 people
for 2400 bucks, 480 apiece—less
than a stereo, less than season tickets to the Mets.

The Daily News Headlines, 5/24/2000:
> *POPPOP POPPOP POPPOP POP BOOM*
> *SHOT HIM RIGHT IN THE BACK OF THE HEAD*
above a photo of a grinning boy in handcuffs.

If the youngest worker weighed 160
he was worth only 3 bucks a pound—
cheaper than a choice cut of beef
or some unusual fruit at the greengrocer.

Slaughterhouses are kinder, killing
stone cold dead at a stroke, no bloody
buddy carrying another up the cellar steps,
no young pair of maimed survivors.

Just meat, stacked neatly
in Wendy's basement freezer.

When Broadway's Gone

Broadway will be different once the money's
gone and the lights dim, once roll gates

close over the dark faces of Gracious

Home and Tasti-D-Lite, Eddie Bauer
and the corner boutique; once the movie

house marquees lose their glittering words

and burnt-out streetlights fail to be replaced.
Broadway will be different once the police

cease their patrols and sanitation

trucks stop rolling through the trash-littered
stickup streets for pickups—Broadway

will not even recognize itself.

People will be different once the money's
gone and we stand in the street without clothing

our fragile, equivalent skins

stripped of their costly emblems
stripped of badges and leather and denim

stripped of all symbols of rank,

those blank checks written against the past.
People will be different once the costumes

tatter and the categories fail, when strangers

can only be known by their love or their lacks:
the offered hand, the turned back, the contact

eye to eye, or not. Naked and recognized. Or not.

Homeboy Wheelies

Young men come of age in Harlem
by learning how to drive
a brand-new Medicaid chair.

It's always the boys, looking so street-cool
you know they weren't born to wheels—
gunshot, stomping, nightstick, knife,

then cuffed all night to the ER gurney,
untreated, unseen—ghetto hospital
mayhem ruling while the split

nerves deaden and freeze, leave slick
crippled brothers popping wheelies
on 116th, 147th, Adam Clayton Powell.

Cavepeople

Did cavepeople rubberneck?
when bones snapped and blood ran
did they group up, clubbed and hairy,
to grunt and gaze, did they

know, back in those wheel-less days
the ways of speculation and conjecture,
was one knuckly index finger, extended,
the prehistoric version of indictment?

Our thalidomide babies are aging, stumps
and flippers wrinkling, their wheelchairs
motorized, their fishy patience at an end.
In which direction would the primitives

be pointing? The finger extended,
or the finger circled back, round
and self-referential? Like a wheel.
Like something they've never imagined.

The Blind Man Shops for Condoms

for Dave Simpson

After I put on the velvet jacket he re-takes
my arm and says *wow,*
your whole personality just changed—

That afternoon, he recited a poem
about buying a box of condoms at 7-11.
No one could be better

at sliding on a rubber in the dark
than a man who lives in nothing else.
How might it feel, making love

to someone with a ten-fingered gaze.

Another Hallway Altar in the Projects

One haggard afternoon lifted its funeral skirts,
tucked a gradeschool girl underneath—
Now you see her. Now you don't:
blood in the hallway again.

Custodian, bring out the homicide mop.

One minute of thrusting.
One busted windpipe, one
pale thimbleful of crackhead semen
(he needed to squeeze his dick into her so bad...)

Project shrines blossom overnight—
photographs and cheap dolls
flicker of votives over stained tiles,
a bloody mop beside the slop sink,

the perfume of ammonia in the air.

Anthony Baez

*Anthony Baez died in 1994, at 29, strangled in a
chokehold by NYPD Officer Livoti after accidentally
hitting the squad car with his football during a game.*

So I squeezed his neck.
I learned it in Academy.
I didn't squeeze too hard, only
hard enough. We had a riot
situation in the street.
I had to gauge—one down?
or a neighborhood in flames?

I'm a cop, not a psychic.
We got our protocols. I only did
what I was taught to do.

Too tight? Too long?
Adrenaline does interesting
things to the mind.

When you're afraid, do you go on automatic?
Or does the world stop for a minute
while you think?

Earthquake Came to Harlem

When earthquake came to Harlem you were sleeping
curled in a lilac fleece in the lilac bedroom two flights
up from the street where a new crack split the gutter and widened,
swallowing two light poles, one fat black sack of recycled trash
and the mailman, who left Westchester too late to snag
one of those blue-and-white trucks. He was angry
about having to walk his tiresome route, angry
when he slid between the brand-new lips of the mouth
that had been Frederick Douglass Boulevard, he took
his anger and a three-wheeled trolley full of junk
mail into the crevice where all of it shattered
against the seventh car of a C-train going down,
not downtown or southbound, just down,
the dead mailman pinned to its back like a 21st-century
Ahab, Moby's metal belly stuffed with doomed commuters.

7:15. Your lilac walls quiver. A bookshelf topples.
The children downstairs scream for daddy,
but daddy isn't home. He's dangling from his seatbelt
in a flipped-over cab on Mermaid Avenue where he,
shielded by the new mosaic of his windshield,
can't see the sidewalk dissolving and thinks
he's been hit by a truck. Or something.
Then something hits him again.

Disobedient Billy

I'm gonna show you what happens
to kids who don't listen, said Gloria,
inviting Billy and his mother to come over.

Billy lives across Coney Island Avenue,
a street so wide he might as well live on the moon.
His building is six stories high and half a block across,
all red brick and turrets. Fifty apartments?
A hundred? Kids in most of them. (Welfare
families, Grandma says, when she catches us
watching them play.) Me and my brother,
Anthony, are the only two kids on this side.

Twin garbage alleys tunnel below the building
like train tracks under a hill. A good place
for a bonfire. From the front bedroom window,
we can see one tunnel-mouth glow.

Billy is a skin-and-bones boy who used to stuff
his shirts with newspaper—*Look! I'm the fat man!*
I'm the fat man!—even though his mother said no.
One night, at the bonfire, all that paper caught.
Billy burned bad, wasn't expected to live.
You see, says Gloria, pouring coffee. *You see?*
Billy's purple neck, thick as my father's thigh,
doesn't bend; his tracheotomy furls and unfurls,
like starfish gills, with every breath.

At night, red light slides across our bedroom walls
whenever trucks leave the corner firehouse.
If I happened to burn, they're only half a block away,
past Brighton Parts and the Rexall drugstore, on our
side of the avenue. They'd be here in a minute.
So fast, my neck might not even get warm.

Billy's mother says it's time for them to go.
Unable to look down, he takes the stairs
like a toddler, one step at a time.

2,748 Heroes + 1 Skeezer

Two million in the bank and that son of a bitch
up in smoke—one man's tragedy is this woman's
dream to the 20th power: those towers
coming down gave at least one scumbag
just what he deserved. Oh—excuse me—
make that "at least one *hero*" please pardon my
Staten Island French. Not one dime for his lower
east side chippie, pushing him to leave me.
Sweetheart, I got your divorce right here,
right next to the plaques and photos and little
urn of girder ash stashed in what used to be "his" den.

Sometimes, I put on my old uniform—
muted colors, small pearl studs, gold locket
on a thin gold chain and the same blank
face I wore all those years he cheated me—
and ferry to the survivor event of the day.

I know to keep my mouth shut, pretend to care
about their statues. You never know,
another check might be dropping in the mail.
Afterward, I ride the boat home to my empty,
mortgage-free house, to days with no more
liar in them, to afternoon Bingo and a scotch.

Or two. One night, when I forgot to let the dog out,
she peed all over my brand-new Italian stone
kitchen floor. On a whim, I sucked up some puddle
with an eyedropper, squirted it into the urn.
Bone dust, burnt girder, poodle piss.
My secret. Mine.

The Microbugs

At last, the nameless microbugs of summer
who seeped, like smoke,

between the inadequate wires of three cheap
Woolworth screens, have ceased their relentless

buzzing and sneaking. Every morning of August
I woke to dotted sheets and shoulders

dusted with microscopic corpses, bodies
crushed by the glance of a thumb,

fold of a pillow, bend of an arm.
Transparent and boneless survivors

dive-bomb the dawn blinds, beat
off into the smudged ozone. A wild flock of angels.

Interior Poured

The moon is empty tonight.
Her rank interior poured itself across
a taut horizon, spread

to mix with the city's dank sweat
and blank cement squares. Men were dying,
but the black rain filled their mouths, muffled their cries.

No angels came to help. The women
brought their buckets and trudged
to where the sea was: a simple treachery

had turned its tides to sand, the land
curdled and stank beneath thick,
pungent layers of moonshit. But she—

empty as a balloon—is smiling in her orbit.
All these years they nourished her with sins.
She talked to herself,

tried not to notice the cramps.
The men just can't believe she couldn't hold it.
They meet in parks at night, and plan for war.

Therefore, she will fill up again,
and those men will be running for cover
when the moon returns their gifts.

Diorama

Ammunition

He keeps it in his sock drawer, underneath the folded hankies
and never leaves the house without it:

even on the beach, my father is armed,
guarding our coolers and blanket.

He cleans it at the kitchen table while arguing with his wife.
At sink, stove, fridge, the weapon tracks her,

oiled white cloth twirling slowly in the barrel,
until her frosted Maybelline mouth closes.

When he finally reloads it, I help, ferrying bullets
one by one from the green glass ashtray

to the center of his smooth white palm.
Eyes steady on Gloria,

he slides the slugs softly into place,
small metallic kisses—

click. click. click.
click. click. click.

The Scissors of My Mother

Five or six times every year we'd re-enact the tragedy of haircut,
where Mom squints over my magazine example,
a Pall-Mall dangling from her apricot mouth,
asking for details she somehow never used.
"That one will be beautiful on you, it frames the face."

The scissors of my mother committed atrocities
like high-water bangs and pointy sideburns,
her sloppy layers like a lopsided chessboard
decades before buzz and fade became styles.
Sobbing in the aftermath, I'd have to hear
how much her customers love the way she does their hair,
the nicest way she knew to call me stupid and ungrateful.

In the magazine still open on the table,
a babe in a feathery shag tosses her head.
I tear out the page, ball it in my fist:
"You said you would do *this*."
"Don't holler at your mother," she tells me,
"I've got more two-dollar tippers than anybody else in the shop."
I had no way to know if that, if anything she said, was true,
no way to repair the damage done. Once again
there will be whispering in the schoolyard
  —looks like foureyes fell asleep under a lawnmower
  —wouldn't you die before you came outside like that?
and my wet eyes red behind thick prescription lenses.
Glasses chosen, as always, by Gloria, cheap brown
octagons too big for my small face. Too much eyeglass,
not enough hair … and nothing much worth framing in the first place.

Old Woes (I)

They tell me I'll be sorry when she's dead, but I don't think so.
I'm worn-out and done, spent on her treasure of miseries.

I used to set down the phone to start a pot of coffee,
her voice a tinny whine on the countertop as I measured and poured

—listening isn't on her agenda, and nothing she tells me is new.
I could leave the receiver right there, forever,

let Gloria spew her old woes to my old stove.
Who knows? She may never even notice that the audience is gone.

Bensonhurst, 1971

Get out and don't come back, she hollers
and I call my mother's bluff, grab a jacket,
slam out the door. 10pm on a school night.

I like walking. First down Benson Avenue that
always smells green, as if freshly mowed,
to the Bay by EJ Korvette's. I watch the ocean
from a bench, breathe tar and salt, kick the fat
water-rats away when they get too close.

Up Bay Parkway to 86th Street, the "Avenue":
a long glass storefront wall under the El,
B trains overhead loud as the end of the world.
I stop in front of Something Else, remembering
when they caught me with a brand-new pair
of elephant bells folded underneath my shirt.
I look into every store window, all that stuff
I can't have. Block after block of it.
The tracks follow me south to Stillwell Ave,
split off right before the high school.

It might be getting close to morning. I see
a hint of navy-blue at the end of Avenue U.
Spumoni Gardens is closed, their picnic
tables still out front as usual. Just past the last
bench, some guy in a long raincoat passes me
from behind, slows, turns, asks the time.
I tap my empty wrist and keep on walking.
He cocks his head, falls into step beside me.
I don't have the time, I say, still tapping.

He puts his arm around me, says he's got a knife.
My brain starts rhyming: knife/time ... knifetime,
as I'm stuffed under his armpit. He's that tall.
He says *Just stay quiet and it'll be all right.*
The rhyme stops. He's steering me off the Avenue.

What street is this? 10th? They're all the same around here.
Narrow driveways. Gravel, grass, gravel. Jesus, rosebushes,
an ugly concrete birdbath. His arm is high around my face—
if not for the coat, I could bite the crook out of his elbow.
The trim, grim Home Ec teacher pops into my head.
Say you're sick, say you're pregnant, she taught us.
Don't scream or fight if the man has a weapon.

He makes a hard right toward a driveway. I twist
out of his armpit, say *No! I've got the clap!* finally trying
to run. Not two steps, he's got me back. He ... chuckles?
You gone go make me take out my knife, little miss.
Little miss? *Fuck you!* I push at him and the voice
goes steel: *Make another move like that I'mma cut you.*
He slaps the raincoat around my head, bends me almost double.
Turns us. I hear a click, then

                              I'm on my back in grass.
He shoves my head under a bush. The raincoat slides away.
That green smell. Legs pinned between his knees.
His hands at his belt. A noisy buckle.
I try to sit up. He elbows me down.
My cheap jeans snap open with one rough tug.
I cross my legs tight as I can.
He's never getting these pants off me. Never.

One big hand grabs both ankles, lifting.
Another grabs the back of my pants,
yanks them off my hips. He covers my mouth,
leans on my face—heavy, heavier—then
one stroke BAM he rams his dry cock up my ass.

The pain is psychedelic—flashing lights, a flat buzz in my ears, that harsh
back-throat keening, like in dreams where you can't get the scream out.
Every slam hammers my head into the wooden roots.
He splits my legs over his shoulders and holy shit goes harder

then he's done, just like that. Drops me,
tucks himself in. My hands are freezing.
Count to 100, else I be right back with this here knife.
Footsteps, fast, fading. He's gone. I don't scream.
I would feel stupid, screaming now. Like a liar.
I wipe the blood off my ass with some leaves,
leave the backyard quietly. That click I heard—
before everything—must have been this gate-latch.

Another mile walk, back the way I came. Slower.
The sky's getting light. I turn left, ring a bell.
Theresa makes coffee while I clean myself up.
I drink it standing. She knows about being raped.

Theresa says our Home Ec teacher is a moron:
You told him the clap so you got it up the ass.
I look past her, at my jacket on the doorknob.
*But shit, the way you go for those black guys
you mighta liked it if he put it in the right place.*
Then, her husky voice serious and low,
she says I better not tell anybody. *Well,
not anybody else. You know I would never.*

We were best friends. We were 14. It was Brooklyn.

46

Turning Sweet 16 in Prison

No candles for me: think bigger.
Think high white walls and grated
windows, rings of keys at ignorant waists,
a metal grid to break the dark between my moon and me.

In dreams I soar, fierce at my own controls,
the roar of nighttime traffic down Spofford Ave
receding as I rise, a teenage ring of concentric furies.

When you grow up, Gloria said, as if placing
her curse on me, *I hope you have one just like you.*
But I'd rather fly than replicate—

jettison the uninvited from my womb
and rev the copter's engines. Up.
Up, over and out.

Terminatrix

Swirls of steel, blood
spinning into a tube.

My body recalls the swell of early
milk, doubletalking

heartbeats, the way baby
things in shopwindows shook

off their saccharine
and briefly glowed.

A woman takes the empty
seat beside me on the subway.

There are other seats—
why here? I slam

through the steel connecting door
into another car, leave

plenty of room
for her and her stroller.

Wallpaper

One day Mom gives me a diet pill so I can help her tear the old kitchen wallpaper down. What wallpaper has to do with dieting I don't know, but in an hour we're working like demons. She's got two-three Pall Malls going at a time, I'm drinking soda after soda and chewing the insides of my mouth to bloody shreds. We get that wallpaper down, all right, it takes about twelve hours of steady teeth-grinding work but we finish it and at 9pm we're still ready for more so we each take another diet pill and stay up all night pasting brand-new turquoise-flowered vinyl to the walls. I'm just an assistant, of course, Mom is the home improvement genius, but what an assistant I am. She can hardly need a thing without me already having it in my hand, ready to pass up through the late-night cigarette mist to my laddertop mother while I jitter from leg to leg.

I go to sleep at dawn, wake up at noon, Dad's been home and gone out to his second job already. I'm exhausted, my mouth so sore I can barely drink a cup of coffee. Mom doesn't look very good, but she's happy because Dad loves the new wallpaper. The kitchen is gorgeous, bright and alive as I felt after the first diet pill yesterday morning. When Mom leaves for Bingo I ransack her dresser, night table, sewing kit, finally find bottles of the green-and-white capsules in an old pocketbook on the floor of her walk-in closet. I only steal two. Capsules, not bottles. Not yet.

One Perfect Lemon

An orderly room surrounds her
the way the setting of a well-planned suicide

surrounds its corpse. She's still breathing,
thrusting, hopeful,

through the gelid snowdrifts
that constitute her days. Still life, with snowshoes.

Or a landscape that no one has offered to paint.
She is a lemon—

a bad model.
Lemon sounds better: some people like them,

swallow them almost whole, stuffing tart
yellow segments into their mouths

like candy, noses
wrinkled against the pleasurable sting.

She is waiting to meet a lover of fine old lemons.
She is waiting.

Gloria's Favorite Appliance

One more shining thing to put in the shiny kitchen: a closeup
makeup mirror, double-sided and edged
with discs of relentless light: switch it on and voilá—
your face becomes a moonscape of nostril and pore.

I liked me better reflected off the table,
checkerboard cheeks, checkerboard forehead
frowning up from the smooth Formica.

I could even see myself in the linoleum after she mopped,
trapped cross-legged in my spot between radiator and stove
while she hollered about the foyer not being dry yet.
When I looked up from the coloring book,
there it was again: my blurry face,
floating on the polished oven door.

Weren't there enough copies of us in here already?
Dad said we were paying Clairol's mortgage.

She never turned the mirror on when he was home,
never unplugged it or took it off the table when we ate.
Even with its shutters latched, the makeup mirror threatens,
like McGready's German shepherd down the street,
chained to a stake in the old man's alley—
always snarling, always just about to get free.

Shutting Down

The white brick wall around the building
in the photo captioned *Spofford Shutting Down*
goes eleven feet over ground level, and the roll gate
on the left is the entrance to the subterranean garage.
This is where they wrangled us in, on the bus, cuffed
and sometimes shackled, peering through steel window grilles
at the blank white face of our new home. I remember
the bar-crossed view from my cell overlooking the courtyard
where we were brought out for afternoon walks and a smoke,
and how they clipped our doled-out cigarettes in half, as punishment.

That summer Dad caught me out in Steeplechase Park,
and dragged me home to my grandmother's apartment.
"Now she's kissing niggers," was all he said before it started.
At the hospital I was treated, interviewed, released;
Dad was handcuffed, interrogated, uncuffed, released;
my mother declined to press charges. A few weeks later
she swore out a PINS, Person In Need of Supervision,
put me away for the crime of being more than she could handle.
I was shipped straight to prison from the courtroom, numb,
the white of my left eye still red, arms and thighs the purple
of eggplant, skull lumped and swollen, both eye sockets black.
I let everybody think other cops had done it to me,
said I was arrested for assault, never mentioned the boy.

In my first week at Spofford Hall I learned how to snap
two teeth off a cheap plastic comb, shove it up a cigarette
and smoke it for the buzz, just like sniffing glue. Learned
how to fight back and how to do time. Learned how nothing
seemed to hurt much after those hours in Grandma's spare room,
the repetitious thuds of pistol hitting skin, head hitting wallboard,
the sour smell of Johnny Walker Black.

These days, I hardly ever think about the night my father almost killed me
or the whole long locked-up summer afterward when I wished that he had
or how it all went from bad to worse to utterly impossible
when the D.O.C. bus slid behind those high white walls
and my unfathomable mother wiped her hands.

Ensign Chekov

Star Trek ca. 1970

I never heard anything like the way he talked.

As if his mouth was filled with tiny porcupines
that terrorized his tongue, forcing it to excavate
words straight from the adam's apple through
the left bow of his half-lifted lip.

He showed up every night but never stayed long,
a minute or three twirling dials and frowning at his monitor
in that tight red shirt, the one I wanted to wriggle him out of.
He never looked at me, while I invented words for the brown
of his big, uncatchable eyes: cinnaleather, woodstar, besmoked.

When I forgot how to sleep I imagined him saying my name—
Mary Ann—his glottal Y merging the vowels of Mary.
Meghyaaaan. I barely recognized myself in the two
syllables of this new name, the one my mother takes four
to say, the name I fled at seventeen when I fled them all.

In the apartment that we always called our house
life was lived by interruption: furniture smashed, bottles
shattered, telephones flung, squad cars at the curb
and both generations screaming—sometimes all at once.
Mary AAA-aan, who never seemed to get things done quite right,
was summoned a hundred times a day—from the kitchen
or loudly off the terrace, the whole neighborhood glancing
up at the strident knell of Gloria's elongated singsong.
Mary AAA-aaan! You get upstairs right now!

Meghyan is soft. Slurred. A girl someone might even...desire.
I pictured my fingers on his throat, just above the crewneck collar,
touching his voice as it thrummed. The warm engine of an idling
bus at the Bensonhurst depot briefly rechristened for Jackie Gleason.
I was long gone by then, saw the brass sign years later,
a rare visit to Bay 38th Street, scene of so many old crimes.

Jackie Gleason would have loved our old terrace.
I bet he would've used it the way my mother did—
sent Alice loudly to the moon every night,
right there, the whole neighborhood listening.

Gloria's Stories

My mother talks the way flea-bitten dogs scratch their itching
flanks: without thought; without shame, without cessation.

Because of her, I know the size and strength of my father's cock
and that he never went down on her until after the divorce.

I know the consistency of my grandmother's shit, have heard
a hundred times what it's like to wipe her blistered crack.

Stopped mid-sentence, she says *"What's the matter,
you don't want to talk to your mother?"*

She and I, she and everyone,
have been having this same conversation for decades.

In the mythology of Gloria, life is peopled with undoers
who shield her from happiness the way shutters

block the daylight from a room. And there she stands,
powerless, at a window she would never think to open for herself.

I'm a big star in Gloria's story, the wicked young witch who
wouldn't even take her own mother in: at last,

she's gotten something right—like that itchy, scratching dog,
its restless claws finally hitting the sweet spot.

Dad's Last Wife

Before the fat woman started to die
I could not like her. Mismatched place settings
extracted her contempt like a tap
pulling syrup from a tree—things
I never noticed or, noticing, ignored.
But not around Carol. *This is good enough
for you,* her eyebrow queried while
swapping platters, *this is how you like to live?*
I tolerated her rearrangements in silence,
helped re-set the set table, did not sigh out loud.

The last round of chemo left her hairless as a baseball.
I helped her to the bathroom, held her naked head
over the sink, squeezed a shoulder when it heaved.
My father stayed in the kitchen, matching up plates
and laying the table with food that Carol could not eat.
She pretended, rearranging sandwich meats until
we could almost believe she'd gotten something down.

After lunch, a neighbor came to visit.
Carol brought an empty casserole to the loveseat—
"Just in case," she said—and sat, rose-patterned
china in her lap, head now fashionably turbaned in silk.
Dad offered around coffee and cake, Carol
pointed at the basin and shook no. Then she laughed,
the furious laugh of cancer, and said "My God,
isn't this classy?" That's when I understood
the power of placemats, matching silver,
napkins folded like birds.

My Father on Life Support

A catheter extends from the noisy million-
dollar machine at the foot of his bed to the pump
installed beside his heart, which is "resting".

The pump is loud, relentless—
a click track pacing the rhythm
of my father's pushed blood; the respirator's
rigid tube distends his mouth into a grin.

I've taped a smiling picture of Dad above
what may well be his deathbed. *"Call me George!"*
is scribbled across the bottom in blue magic marker.
The ICU nurses like this portrait, and stop saying Mr. Jaccarino.

Years ago, my father sang along with Aqualung
and Locomotive Breath, fingered flute solos
in the fragrant air above our griddle. Now,
he speaks the garbled tongue of intubation,
a language no one in the ICU can understand.

I swab his peeling lips with glycerine, slather
organic Chapstick all over his mouth.

"Five days," says Dr. Vasavada. "That's the max."
Then this universe of interventions must go dark.
And dad's battered heart will beat alone. Or not.

Old Woes (II)

My mother sits, as always, across from the cheap TV
but what she's really watching is the past.

In her bedroom, a regiment of plaster saints
dominates a dressertop littered with votives and photos.

Jude, the saint of hopeless cases, is her patron.
Like everyone else, he has failed her—

never earning his place among the candles.
Who will restore the gone years?

She deserved better. She still does.
She turns up the television, waiting for something to happen.

At the Office

I listen to the music of his work
—the giant insect drill and blood-
chilling gargles of the patients—

read outdated magazines
in waiting-room suspense.

A snug-uniformed secretary
touches up her lipstick
behind the frosted glass:

I hate her for calling me in.
Dentists dwell at the hairline

between requisite pain and prodigal
cruelty. When Doctor Klaus
lanced the un-numbed abscess

bulging the roof of my adolescent mouth
I didn't understand that he had choices.

Thirty years later, Dr. H
leads me to a chair. His treatment room
reeks of old silver, loud water

spins pointlessly in a bowl,
instruments glide overhead

primed to suction out
or bore into. I take
the patient's position,

open wide at his command,
my mouth already filled with shadows.

An Address I Could Never Find Again

What I didn't like about the kiss
in the dark at an address
I could never find again
was the rush of invisible
mouthwash breath against my face.

After traveling alien subway lines all night,
we let them turn off all the lights.
I don't remember his name or where we met them,
which girlfriend I was with
and whether or not the one I got was cute.

Just that fragrant mouth
pursuing me through the black
muscle of unfamiliar city air.
We left, and I thought I was going home
but I haven't made it home in more than thirty years.

Home is a white canopied bed,
a cheap white gold-printed desk,
a mangy dog snapping in the driveway
and the comforting smell of fear
on the stove with the bacon.

My key no longer fits that lock.
I am left instead with decades
more of aimless subway travel,
the paychecks and tax forms,
a plot or an urn.

Send me out onto the beach.
Let there be Tuesday night
fireworks in Brooklyn once again
rockets exploding in violet and red,
the cool sand cradling my head.

Diorama

Somewhere outside, Johnny Tango was waiting.

Mom kissed us both, said *"I'm going to the bakery.*
Watch your baby brother for me." At six, I was the big one.
She smelled of lipstick. Then she was gone.

We stayed at the kitchen table, working on a shoebox
diorama. Cutout people. Cotton-ball clouds.

The snow came down and came down.
After awhile, we needed the kitchen light—
standing on a chair, I just reached the pull-chain.

Our phone sat on a blond-wood table by the castro
where my parents slept. I picked it up and dialed zero,

listened to it ring. *"Operator, I think my mother*
fell down a snowhole." I was proud
to know the answer when she asked for our address.

I pressed my face hard into the bedroom window,
saw the snow still falling, the brown clothes-
line gone soft and white, the windowsill
capped in clean silver triangles of ice.

It was almost dark when the doorbell rang.
Two policemen came up the stairs.
Not Mom. Not Dad, in his own blue uniform.
Not Grandma, tired from work, rolling rubberbands
off the dark top edge of her A&S stockings.

I answered questions—
      the bakery on Avenue U
      Daddy's at work
      Grandma's usually home by now
      no, nobody called
      I don't know
      I can't tell time yet
—while the other cop looked around.

"Listen to me. There's nothing to be scared about.
Your mom had something to take care of. OK?
Why don't you kids show us what you're making?
That thing on the kitchen table."

    If someone had told me the truth:
      that my father was at his girlfriend's place
      that my mother left us for her dance teacher
      that the dance teacher would turn out to be a pimp
      that Dad would find Mom in a Manhattan bar 2 months later
    I wouldn't have understood a word.

I told the cop it's called a diorama.

Solo

To Xerox Three Stapled Sheets:

is simple—separate
and lay the pages flat, shut
the lid, press a switch.

But who am I
to rip that staple out?
Twelve years have passed since she died

and maybe these pages
are the last of all the pages
stapled by my friend in her truncated life:

three old poems on onionskin
that rolled off an Olivetti in the seventies.
To leave them uncopied is to soon

lose them altogether; to take them apart
is to yank the silver keystone from a mortarless wall,
the small metal stitch

that pins her soul to the world.
Prying open staplejaw, I feel
the hushed breath of her rush past, see a riot

of lilacs nodding on her dresser
in our rented Brooklyn rooms, smell
the brown hair at her neck.

And I dip down, deep,
into the quivering sweat
of memory, consume this

heady oddity of bliss, allow her
to inhabit the air beside me
as the unclenched staple drops.

Getting Everything I Did & Didn't Want

I wanted all of you, even—maybe especially—the bad parts; dark and pliant as the sweet black bruises on a roughly-handled piece of fruit.

I wanted your wisecracks about Disney, patron saint of rehabs, and to hear you say "sick as a broke-dick dog."

I wanted your blue eyes, your prison record, your size 15 sneakered feet.

I wanted your wife to leave or die, and when she did I wanted you reading with me on the futon, one leg slung over mine, your Kool simmering in our ashtray, your corduroy shirt hung from the cut-glass knob of the French door.

I wanted to climb through windows with you, get arrested with you, leave court at 4am with you and try to cop a bundle in the blizzard, our gloveless hands wet and cold around the very last money on earth.

I never wanted to be homeless with you, share your welfare card, teach you to beg on the subways. Finally I wanted to lose you but didn't know how.

You disappeared and I wrecked the cassettes. Unraveled every celluloid imitation of your voice.

Three years clean and I wanted to kill you, but I never wanted your mother's call telling me you'd done that already, yourself.

Flamingo Corduroy

This Sunday is vacant as Dougie's old corduroy shirt, vacant and long as the XL sleeves that have hung empty in my closet since before he opted out. The shirt's lived with me longer than he ever did. I still smell him in its faded rose folds, still see his giant hands dangling preposterously from the frayed pink cuffs. Can almost feel those hands wrapped around my face.

It was his favorite shirt, a bright pink contradiction, girly-colored cotton sliding over jailhouse tattoos, two top snaps separated by the golden bulk of his tracked neck, that place I used to kiss before the scabs and the keloid scar.

When is a long time long enough? His teenage Navy picture on the bookcase, a snapshot of his headstone in an envelope, his bones in the ground down south somewhere, courtesy of a born-again Christian who planted old stumblebum junkie dad right in her own backyard.

Yearning Looms Huge

When one yearns for one
who wants one not
at least one has that yearning.

A yearn, though unreturned,
occupies the heart's apartments—
that heart abandoned

when yearn dissolves.
One imagines yearnless life
improves upon a life of yearn

unrequited, but no—unoccupied
by any body of desire, the heart
must yearn to yearn again.

At Daiuto's

I asked her, "Is this a date?"
while I wrestled with the bento box, an embarrassment of food
across from her vegan rice and salad.

She had on the usual sleeveless black top, bare
freckled biceps white as the paper cover on our table,
white as her legs that I hadn't yet seen.

I kept my eyes off her face, grateful
that my fish kept slipping off the lacquered
chopsticks, something to fuss with

in case she thought I was joking. In case she laughed.
But no. Like a zen monk, the Sicilian girl gives
question for question, says, "Do you want it to be?"

She's 28 years old, sexier than her poems.
She knows what I want and what she can have,
gets to decide what will or won't be received.

I just nod, like a hinge-headed puppy in the rear-view.
I don't remember who spoke next or what was said.
I only remember that this was how we started.

If I'd paid more attention that night
to how skillfully she held her cards,
their regretful slow-motion drop,

one by one, onto the table; if I'd noticed how
still she kept her face, the way her eyes
stayed only on my mouth,

I would have thanked her for a pleasant dinner,
taken care of the check,
and gone home alone for the next two years.

Unwritable

In the single-minded
pursuit of grammatical
exactness, a poem was lost:
slipped off in a red mess of carets,
extractions, commas.

Perfectly correct,
out of error and out
of breath, the poem passes
academic muster and takes its
lackluster place in the stacks.

Flat precision of subject, object, tense.

I am nothing
but a tense myself.
I tense for you.
I lie in wait to lay you down.
I lay in wait to lie with you.

And if I said *we lied together*
where one wrong word links
sex and betrayal in a single
tense syllable, how much
crimson ink would it take

to fix this unrightable wrong?

The New Yorker Fashion Issue

They strike me hard tonight, those sexy girls
gripping cell phones and voluptuous

decanters of cologne in their perfect fingers,
posing moist and open-mouthed, as if another

tongue flicked across the plump low
lips beneath their Prada hems and slim

lace slips—the best lick
coming just as the camera-eye winks.

Poem for a Moment of Depression

I don't want to write anything. I would prefer
        to be a rock shining at the waterline, soaked in sea-
        spray, motionless as Buddha. I would prefer the
        silences of space far beyond the place of telescopes
        and radio waves. I would prefer to be finished.

I do not want to
        brew any more pots of coffee, fill out any more tax
        returns, brush any more teeth.

I do not want to
        scrub the toilet, walk the dog, make a date, strip,
        fuck, suck, walk, talk, pretend, embellish or eat.

And I will not apologize.

Enough

sometimes warm stone is enough
my back in a thin t-shirt against the April wall
where sun has worked its heat all afternoon
and rough brick resists my leaning weight
I love how it doesn't move, how I can count on its indifference

sometimes watching the mouth of a stranger is enough
I don't even have to touch it, slide my finger along a lip
or let it dampen the side of my face
I only want to witness the dark of it
that tongue undulating in its cage of teeth
the slick spit gleaming

the kiss that doesn't quite happen interests me most
twin mouths trading nothing more than breath
as if kissing would cancel the hungers
I need to know everything about not having

there's a silver earring in the street
misshapen by tires or heavy heels
I peel it off the sweating tar, tangled and bright
a beauty that doesn't know it's shattered
that glimmers in my hand, like a cripple flaunting her strut

I straighten the warped earpiece
and the pleasure of fixing this twisted thing
shows me how I might sometime be loved
imperfect woman on a warm brick wall
just shining there, just waiting to be found

Solo

I've lived by myself since 1993, cracking
jokes about the singular life:
my way of whistling past the graveyard.

In the beginning, I felt freed—
no more lies, no more toenails
in the bathroom sink, plenty of milk
for morning coffee. But now,

I'm playing a solo when I want a duet
and sometimes I think anyone would do.
Other times, no one. I haven't sculpted

a space in my days for a lover to slide into
because I don't want to watch it while it's empty,
like sleeping every night beside a ghost,
or setting an extra cup on the table

for the absent guest, like a Passover jew.
It's easier to act as if my private music has absorbed me.
As if I wouldn't have it any other way.

Dominant Hand

with thanks to Marie Howe

In beauty culture school, when I swapped
the manicure scissors from left hand to right on my first
real-live volunteer customer, two senior students
goggled at me, like parents seeing their little girl
in makeup for the very first time.
"How did you do that?" the cute one asked.
"Do what?" I said. "Do what?"

Ambidextrous with silverware, razors,
screwdrivers and paper-clips, I'm still
labeled a lefty because of the way that I write.
Yet there are two things that my left hand
cannot do. One of them is strum a guitar.
The other also involves strumming—
no instrument required.

Sheep's Meadow

I spread my arms while thunder
crashes around me like an angry neighbor.
Not one raindrop

has fallen yet to signal the onslaught
that I alone, here in the treeless bowl
of Sheep's Meadow at midnight, know is coming.

It's one thing to be alone in the dark.
It's another thing to be alone in the dark in the rain.
And it's something else entirely

to be alone in the dark in the rain in the middle
of the city's most threatening park.
I'm thinking of you, of the oxygen tongues

forcing themselves from their silver tanks and down
past the familiar lips, the teeth, down
your throat and into the smoke-broken lungs

somewhere nearby, in an adjustable
hospital bed. You. At least the storm
erases with its clamor the hissing of your tanks,

washes with its drops the drip-drip-dripping
down a tube, through a needle, into you.
Flowers browning on your windowsill, a new

magazine, candy bars no longer allowed,
visitors limited, hours limited, I am limited—
I am alone in the New York dark,

waiting for a storm in Central Park
and when the rain comes finally slashing down,
I will thank it for the company.

In My Cell

The body takes eleven months
to regenerate every living cell.

All I have to do is wait
while progressive time incubates
a person who has never held you.

Skin cells slough away quickest:
already the pores of my face have been made new.

The cells of heart and brain
buried deep in bloody cavities
take longest to die off.

They remember you.
They last and last.

Dream Me Coupled

Think of me, when you think of me,
as the wisecracking weaver in the back of every room
who wove a sling of jokes to hold your tears

on the morning you were bereft. Think of me
as a book you might not read, an unframed
poster long unhung, the one broken
button on your stereo remote.

Never think of me, though, as unloved—
that's my job, and I do it well:
wandering unpeopled rooms to name
the missing, the unmet, the dead.
Yet every now and then think me

paired, matched, partnered; conjure
one shape to place beside me in your sleep
and dream, dream me coupled—the permanent half
of something much, much larger: not a third,
not a quarter, not an all-enduring
unremarkable whole.

So think of me, when you think of me,
if ever you should think of me at all,
as anchored, rooted, cherished—
not a wet-eyed smiler on the stony brink
but a blank screen during intermission,
before the personalities of light.

Infant Face of Desire

I shred my affirmations daily, feed
scribbled-over index cards

into a tiny machine:
destruction is the only cure for secrets—

like burning a wish to make a smoke
that reaches the nose of heaven.

What I want
is unmistakable light, a sourceless

voice that speaks my private language:
interpreter of heartbeat,

eyeblink, breath.
I settle at the outermost edges of wanting,

blank as an infant that doesn't know
a thing about desire

but waits (wide-
mouthed) for nothing in particular.

Pickup Line

Lunchbucket on a dungaree lap, he looked up
from his roast beef and his rye bread, his mayo
and his day-old beard, he looked up and said *Lady*...

I slowed down to listen, turned my head, didn't quite stop.
Sandwich suspended between his knees—handsome and
unsmiling—he said, *If I was a girl, I'd wanna look just like you.*

This happened in another time. When being online
meant standing at a Bohack checkout, and girls were measured by the gifts
their men had given: an ankle bracelet, a wedding ring,

a silver picket fence. My odd-looking young self yearned
for features blank as Barbie's. For a motionless styrofoam face
something like a wigstand. Counting flaws in the morning mirror,

I ran out of fingers to tally my lacks: Eyes too close.
Mouth too narrow. Neck too short. Chin too long—
long list of features which never did/never would fit

the blueprints found in holy Seventeen and holy Cosmo.
Exhausted by this lost-cause emulation, I emptied the bulging bathroom cabine
of lacquer / gloss / pencils / powder, set my scrubbed face

loose from its daily precision of paint. And sent it naked into a world
where it cost nothing to delight me: one pickup line from a workman,
sitting in some doorway with his lunch.

Playground of Face

As soon as I learn to love my face
it changes—new droop, new line,
new dark angle under the long bone.

Midlife days pass the way fearless
children pass through a sandbox, leave
kneeprints and fingerholes, crisp furrows

trailing the slide of a daredevil foot.
No one comes around any more, at night,
to smooth the sand

but I don't mind.
Let those leaping hours
leave their message on me.

Reborn at Lenscrafters

yesterday I bought me some blue eyes
not the bright ghost-eye pale baby blues of my brother but deep sapphire eyes
midnight in the cathouse eyes staring from a trailer door
or a dark little bar on Route 17 with a solid beercap wall
and a solemn guy asking if you'd like another round
but that's not where I am—not in the cathouse
or the trailer and especially not the bar *(even though*
I'd like another round—God yes!—a bottomless round)

instead, I'm drinking coffee in the middle of my life
hair all thready with silver, more like a tweed skirt than a skunk
silver goes well with my navy blue living-room walls
like on my brother's beautiful face, his gray temples matched so perfect
with his baby blue little brother eyes, those eyes he's had since he was zero
I always wanted them, back when we were playing Skelly and watching cartoons
or robbing the landlord and getting thrown out of school
I wanted those big blue eyes that made women line up ready to die for him

Bartender, bring me a round of sapphire eyes.
Lens solution on the side please. No ice. Thank you.

I promise I'll carry them well, like a thing I've always had
like my heart that always beats the same no matter what
I'll carry them the way those impossible shining black women
carry gourds full of water on their heads with never a drop spilled down
and I'll watch all those dull-eyed years dissolve—
quenched and drenched in the brand-new blue-eyed personhood of me

Dream Eyes

Why is it that only eyes are ever
called hazel? Bruises can be hazel,
yet they're called black-and-blues
even when they aren't, even after they've

yellowed like the topaz eye of a cat.

Witch-hazel isn't hazel, it's clear as vodka,
but a good thing to rub into your hazel-colored bruise.
Your bruise, I said, not your pretty hazel eyes.

Close them now, it's time to sleep.
Not read, not play scrabble on the phone,
but sleep. If rough dreams wake you red-eyed

remember why God made Visine.
Soothe your whites, then strut
those hazels out into the varicolored day.

Another Way to Write about the Body

It's nothing but an enemy:
this chubby husk with its lust

for inebriants and drama, its shabby
teeth and sheath of biodegrading skin—

a tiresome history in scars.

This is no silhouette to savor
or love, but a sack of cracked brick to toss

into the nearest, deepest lake
and let sink, gradual as pregnancy,

shocked numb in a slow-motion plummet

through water of ice, water of wind-
pipe and lung: let it be slung

down to the muddy bottom
where every body's welcome waits and let

the weight of it come off of me at last.

Alien Periscopes

Most days I wake up grateful for having been born
without a periscope between my legs,
rising (or failing to rise)
as it chooses, as if

it weren't a part of my body at all
but the remnant of some alien mind
peering out through my eyes to snatch
glimpses of unsettling red lipstick, sheer

pantyhose painted over tanned legs,
the clench of a waist, shake
of an ass, the dark and inaccessible
depths of passing cleavage.

Tasteless and indiscriminate,
the alien lifts and nags: never limited
to faces or bodies, stiffening at a glimpse

of pistols and train wrecks,
jump shots and touchdowns,
thoughts of capture or escape.

Most days I wake up grateful
for having been born without one of these:
boners, woodies, hard-ons,
the Pied Piper of body parts

busy as a lie detector in a humming house of thieves—
up and down, up and down; reacting, reacting
to stimuli piped in from everyfuckingwhere
with no time off for sleep or good behavior.

Boygirl

She always said she was the boy—
I didn't know it meant she'd leave like one,
swagger through the wreckage behind her affair
with an unfond farewell and two dozen unreturned calls.
She always said she was the boy—
even though I'm the one who showed up
with the strap-on, stiff, under my zipper.

She stripped and spread, giggling, girlish.
I lowered over her, dipped in. Again. Again.

Two months after the split, I still find long
strands of hair curling at the baseboards,
smudges of her secret eyepencil edging the vanity mirror.
I kept her cards and letters, the photos, our dick.
She kept her dwindling heart, found another box
cold enough to keep that sorry thing alive: slow
beats of hypothermia doled out like her miserly love.

She always said she was the boy—
squeezing her two faces into my life
then pulling them out quick: love-us interruptus,

a cunt's-eye example of hard-hearted malehood—
handsome outside, poisoned inside:
just the kind of boy I would never lay myself down with, never again

Bikini Line

It wasn't tenderness, but business.
An unexpected

bonus in met flesh, her hand
hard against that spot no hand has touched

since the last love left my universe, laughing.
Competent and stern

she sweetened my creases
with powder, then spread the hot

wax, wooden paddle
dipping and layering

like a chef at work on a cake.
First it was a wrist, angled against me,

as she set the cheesecloth strips in place.
Then the startling

heel of her right hand, dead
center, my sudden swelter rivaling the high

liquid heat of the wax as she stripped off the cloth,
yanked out all my wayward strands and pulled

her pressing hand away:
too quickly to discover what I had no way to hide—

how the body welcomes every gift.
How it glistens and quivers

without question—whether touched
by purpose, or touched by chance.

My Enemy

Runaway: 3 Weeks Later

Two cops, ununiformed, crept up
tenement steps at 2am. They knocked,
nose-up weapons cocked, at the topmost door.
The younger one was my father.

I'd never seen him move like that,
spinning silent with his gun into the hall.
Lights went on in rooms I couldn't see.
I heard shouts. I heard doors slam.
I heard the scrape of a shoved bed.

Somehow, nobody got hurt that night.
Nobody was high enough to argue,
nobody was high enough to reach
for the weapon in their pillow—no.
They just let me go.

Meeting Patti Smith in Brooklyn

I was a weird kid, did weird things, the boys on the corner
made weird-girl jokes about me. All of them were true.

One afternoon, at Slats' house (her furious
mother hollering, as usual, downstairs), stereo

cranked and trembling, we discovered the power of weird
in a little-girl street voice that swiveled around to speak

with itself, cursing what it would curse, hurling mysterious
lyrics into the humdrum air of a Brooklyn apartment. The mother

nearly lost her mind: we played Land so many times
our hands could find the right groove on the record

without looking, even as stoned as we were.
How many hours had passed? Enough to blow through a lid

of Mexican Green, enough for the sun to disappear, enough
to read every word on the album cover twenty times over

and run our fingers again and again across Patti's black
jacket and spotless shirt, across her face, mesmerized and unashamed.

This wasn't music, it was permission—a bomb blasting *should* into shre
We walked into Slat's pink poster-covered bedroom

two nerdy girls who never could never would fit in,
and walked out of it women who didn't want to.

4517 Carlyle Road, Santa Clara, CA

If Escher dreamed in cream and beige
his stairwells rising and falling without end,
neither a climber nor a crumb upon them,
he would dream this antiseptic place of hidden
keys and multiplied gates, a fortress
disguised as gingerbread house.

I yearn for a misdrawn line, some
comforting disorder to prove
that humans live here.

Smoking on the immaculate balcony,
stealthy as a thief, I watch the rain
and flick my guilty ashes.
What did I expect? a desk
festooned with Post-Its, a brick of soy milk
curdling in the fridge, a transplanted
version of my little Harlem home?

Winter isn't solemn in New York—
we raise shared brows and shake
our heads about the latest snow, remind
some stranger not to forget his umbrella
when he stands to step off the subway.

Out here, I could step right off the world
without anyone telling me "Watch it!"
Out here, it's as if I already have.

Red Tape

In the projects on Rutgers Street, lower east side,
George shot up some Red Tape dope
and passed out on the shooting gallery floor:

but overdosing doesn't equal automatic death.
Some only die when the body is left
alone, winding down like a tired watch—

if you pick it up and shake it,
the ticking may resume. His breath
was undetectable. Somebody said

      he only shot one bag

while my back-pocket fingers were stroking
five packets of that same dope. I needed to know
how many bags this man had cooked.

So I lifted his face, wiped his drool, pressed
against his mouth, tried to jump-start the suggestion of
a rhythm in his chest, felt him

      rise and fall beneath my pumping hands.

And when he snapped awake, all doped up and stupid,
I extracted facts from him like peanuts from a cracked and dusty shell,
borrowed his belt, shot my cautious quarter-bag, went home.

Twelve people died on the lower east side that weekend,
overdosed on Red Tape dope. Police trolled
slowly down Rutgers Street all Sunday, blasting
warnings from the squad car PAs, keeping their clients alive.
George warned me alive—with the silence of his breath, the blue
ice of his flesh—and as I slammed the ticking back into his heart

       no one could distinguish rescuer from rescued.

Two in the Morning

If I never took off my sunglasses maybe he wouldn't be robbing me now.

The sunglasses are black, reflective, deadly. When I have them on, no one can tell what kind of person I might really be. The Terminatrix.

So while this guy is slipping out his knife, I think about my sunglasses. How maybe if I put them back on he'll get scared and run away.

I go in my jacket pocket to get them. The guy yells, steps forward. My hand comes out with the wallet instead, and a whole fucking two weeks pay. Two dinners in a tablecloth joint? Me and him, wallet and sunglasses? Knife. Adrenaline. Food.

The Only Yellow Thing I've Ever Owned

Ten years ago the Jennifer Leather salesguy gave me a lifetime guarantee:
spill your morning coffee on this sucker, he said (or something very like that)
and nobody would ever know—you'll never have to buy another couch.

Could he tell that I, already past forty, had never bought a sofa
in my life, furnished apartment after apartment with
hauled-up sidewalk leavings and hand-me-downs?

The couch I liked had not-quite-arms that sloped
into the attached cushions like a pair of built-in pillows,
a place to flop and read. No hard edges, no corners,
nothing separate, a thing entire in itself, solid
and contained. The couch came in just a few colors
and, dodging the bachelor-pad cliché of black leather,
I chose yellow. Gulden's yellow yellow, bright and dull.

He was right on the money about that guarantee:
coffee, cherries, diet coke, Chinese food and cheap beer
disappear in a spritz of Fantastic and two swipes of a torn sleeve.

Writing by the window, I sometimes drop my dark-blue felt-
tip pen, and cobalt lightning strikes a mustard field.
The bolt of ink washes away easily as garlic sauce or soda.
Only the charcoal moons along the arm on the side,
where I used to sit when I used to drink, haven't faded out.
Some things are permanent. Other things, not.

Listen to me: I love that fucking couch.

One Uncivilized Soul

Before my husband stepped out of the present tense
we lived in a building that had been left for dead,

walked a wide wooden plank through the window every day
to breathe its rank perfume of rotten plasterboard

and basement dust that rose around our feet.
All night long they'd be calling in the courtyard:

tato bien, street code for safety; or *bajando*,
code for cops and war, while the building

made music out of the dripping of invisible
water and whisper of falling wallpaper peelings, out of

the crunch of crumbs and crack vials between
sneaker and linoleum indelibly patterned with grime.

Squatting there, we learned the worth of cinder blocks and
milk crates, dangled buckets from vertical clotheslines,

buried our shit in the farthest corners, like dogs,
and made sexless junkie love

in the glow of ten-cent bodega candles,
looking almost normal in that cheap light.

In July, when police quarantined the building—
doors and windows sealed in steel,

mattresses and cardboard walls hauled out,
carted off—the husband left without a forwarding address.

For a month I puzzled through the streets,
unable to conjure him out of the sidewalk, sleeping

most nights under a broken ghetto sky
with splintered benches drilling pinholes in my jeans,

homesick for him and the shattered Driggs Avenue rooms.
Such startling loves in the heart of an addict

at the edge of getting free.
Twenty roofed years have folded past me now,

my address taken for granted, my blood
circling through unbruised veins

clean and strong as hydrant water through a hose.
But back there,

in that building, in my mind,
invisible water still drips

basement dust rises
buckets lift to windowsills

and my uncivilized soul
is at home.

Minding the Gap

Loneliness is Brooklyn on Sunday, one
dogwalker weeping down

Coney Island Avenue, her face
a milky blur in the white plate glass of a carpenter shop.

She stops to blot mascara while the terrier whines
and presses forward. This is how her day begins.

Loneliness is a row of empty hangers;
one toothbrush slanted in a blue enamel cup;

snapping awake at sunrise, last night's book
splayed across your chest, the bedside light still burning.

Loneliness is a place on the beach with a sandwich,
watching strangers shake saltwater off their hair—

vigorous as soaked dogs—their naked backs
gleaming with oil applied by familiar hands.

New Yorker Searches for Cigarettes at 6am in Taos

It is the thing that walks, finds its way, has a destination.
It is the thing that walks me, frozen, down gravel roads

where strangers say good morning, oblivious
to numb fingers, wet feet, my easily visible breath

pluming over a measly t-shirt. It will find what it needs,
in this unfamiliar town or any other—mud roads,

highways without sidewalks: no place confounds
this driver with a death grip on the steering wheel of me,

my body nothing more than its vehicle,
a taxi for the thing that walks.

Following Orders

The desk: a black rectangle of gleaming stone, telephone on the left-hand side. No files or pencils or Post-Its or drawers.

Men come in the door across from me. Some nod, most don't, none speak. When they slide their right hands into a slot where the walls meet, an inner door hisses briefly open.

I sit here twelve hours at a time, three times a week, watching the phone. Men arrive singly but often leave in groups of two or three, suit jackets loosened, or looped over their arms, their faces flushed. I can hear their breath.

The first and third of the three calls I took were wrong numbers. On my second call, six months into this assignment, I received instructions: go around to the parking lot and check for a certain plate. The man on the line said he'd hold.

I circled the lot four times, just to be sure. As I turned back toward the windowless building, brushing snow off of my cap, another car arrived and it was the one. I returned to the phone and said, "That car has just arrived, sir. No, sir, he has not yet reached this lobby. You're quite welcome, sir."

As I set down the receiver, both doors opened at once, and for the first time I heard their voices. The newcomer stamped snow off his boots while three men in shirtsleeves held ajar the inner door.

"The whole goddam system is down," said one, jerking his chin toward the scanner, "come on inside." The new man opened his eyes a little wider, took a step backward toward the outside door. One of the shirtsleeve men stepped further into the lobby, slapped him on the shoulder and hug-walked him inside. The steel door hissed shut behind them.

I looked at the steady green ready light on the biometric scanner, waiting for the phone to ring again. Another man arrived, slid his hand into the device. The door slid open as usual.

No one else came or went during my shift. At midnight I turned over the desk and walked out to the lot, saw only tire marks where that car with the certain plate was parked a few hours before.

What's on Sale

"I need a bag of sun," said the red-
headed dad in the plant shop.

"Potting soil's straight back
to your left," the clerk replied.

Sun, soil, light, dark—
wild loose heat in space, the coolness

of bagged loam. Ah, what's
the difference, anyway? Atoms are

composed of mostly nothing, molecules
circling a core that is not there.

Bags of sun, sacks of soil—we all
come for one thing and leave with another.

My Enemy

I know the code words now, all the secret signals of the damned
I have used the knives, climbed in the windows, stretched out my hand
And spent all day waving cardboard at the strangers on the subway
there was nothing left to fear but love

After hating everyone for every dollar in their pocket
Erasing myself on the pages of gotta-gotta-now-now-more-MORE-MORE
I screamed out the name of my enemy, and named my enemy me

And went walking with my enemy, myself, alone
As the lights of the city went off around me
And the light of sanity went off inside me

And I kept my enemy close beside me
Singing her a sweet narcotic lullaby
While we walked without shoes in the rain
there was nothing left to love but fear

So I asked to be rescued, filled out the forms, I sat for the questions
I made up the answers, I took their medicines and pissed into their cups
Hoping for my enemy to die of all this kindness

My wild, careless, howling enemy
A dirty little girl with her toothprints
Right there, in the crook of my arm
Why not curl up, right here, and rest awhile?
I tried for twenty years to kill you, and still you are not dead

So let me wash you, let me feed you, let me take you dancing
Let's get a job, a friend, a tattoo
Something for us, something for me, something for you
there is nothing left to do but love

The Dislodging

I.

I wake to blazing lights, savor
the taste of rescue on my tongue, flavor
of leaked blood and pulled alien bone, ambulance

spinners still reflecting in my brain.
Rushed, guzzling dinner, one slim
bone slipped into my throat where it lodged,

too low, untouchable, invisible, a death-
threat, a mood-change, an instant
shifting of priorities. This was not

the night I had in mind
when I said   *breast and a wing, spicy, no
biscuit, no sides, thanks*   to the Popeye's cashier—

I never envisioned ER klieg lights and name-
tagged interns, never imagined the multi-
tentacled machine doctors

wheeled into my cube five-point-five
hours after that last fast gulp
and the hundred hyper-slow swallows

later on, foreign bone rattling in its narrow
tunnel of throat, each breath
an exercise in terror.

II.

This morning, the Harlem
Hospital emergency room is quiet
and I am no longer afraid. For a few days,

I will remember to take small
bites and chew them. I will recall
the kindnesses and unkindnesses of strangers,

the O-shaped mask taped
between my teeth, the friend
who never arrived.

Chrysanthemum

Vicious flower, your spikes
resemble bloody teeth. Why were you freed from the garden

to track me here, insistent
mill of knifish petals?

I know you creep from the vase, at night
to poison my dreams with war, and the lilies—

quiet and white as nurses—are too polite, too fragile
for anything but retreat.

Silently, they empty from the room.
Chrysanthemum,

your body
hurts me as the world hurts God. I am a lantern[*]

that trims my wick to dim
the spiteful throb of your fuscia light, and lean

toward the lilies that retired,
pale, behind their glass.

But they left no white thing inside this room:
only me, me and my chrysanthemum,

nodding its threatening head before I sleep,
and again, when I rise with a cry at morning.

———————————

* from Fever 103°, by Sylvia Plath

Marlboro Woman

I pass through the spinning glass office doors
picking my way, as usual, between the smokers
busily self-destructing in their ragged grey nicotine shawls
and I remember how *good* that feels.

I started killing myself at twelve
with Mom's Pall Malls and Dad's Lucky Strikes
but I've always been the impatient type.
I needed to kill myself just a little bit faster
found more exotic poisons: cannabis, tuinal, cocaine—
all those complicated scientific names
and then, of course, heroin.

We called it *hair-on* in the ghetto
talking shit while blood dripped to the concrete
of abandoned building alleys from our veins.
I kept my smokes, I kept my cigarettes and reefer,
I kept my beer and my pills and my cocaine
and mixed them all up on the altar of the great god *hair-on*,
a jealous little god who ate all of my friends alive
but still refused to kill me fast enough.

I got so tired of waiting to die that finally I said *fuck it!*
Lost it all, my potions and my powders and my sick
runny-nose mornings in the temple of Lord Jones...
I left a trail of broken spikes and empty cookers
all down the road from subway to rehab
and I never went back—not once—to pick those suckers up.

Now, I work on killing myself only in the most acceptable manner.
Ice-cream. Hamburgers. Subway rides real late at night.
And when I pick my way between the smokers, now,
busily self-destructing in those sweet, sweet nicotine shawls—
I just remember to forget how good that feels.

Repair Job

How many stones fit in a pillowcase?
More than I can carry, fewer than the labyrinth requires.
Walking the rings, I fit stone to gap,

like a dentist furbishing an old mouth,
and run out right away, empty pillowcase
dangling all the long walk out.

This was my first labyrinth. They seemed
ridiculous, unnecessary—I can walk in circles
on my own. Yet, from my second-floor window,

I couldn't follow its turnings by sight.
One morning, with no one around, I tried it.
The maze sucked me under two steps in,

nothing but my feet between stone lines,
nothing ridiculous about it. The next day
I walked it again, noticed how thin

some of the lines were, almost dotted.
The northeast quadrant was worst: yard-long
voids with only a sprinkle of stone

as if someone, seeing the unfilled places,
spread out whatever rocks were handy.
Embarrassing to look at, like

a queen-size woman in a child-sized towel.
After seven trips to the rockpile
my pillowcase is muddy, the labyrinth intact.

The Memory Factory

I am a surgeon for the broken CPUs
working in a scatter of tiny screws
on tabletops littered with dead daughterboards.

I love the feel of wire
sliding through my fingers, that click
when a chip finally locks into its socket, the solid

silicon weight of computer memory held, cautiously,
right in the palm of my hand. Yet even silicon memories may be lost:
when the Singapore factory burned down to the ground

tons of toasted RAM chips flashed out in a sizzle,
billions lost, headline after headline, a catastrophe.
You couldn't get an 8-meg chip for any kind of money.

My own memories go more quietly, taking more with them:
I lose the memory, and the memory of the memory—
couldn't tell you where (or whether) we had dinner last Tuesday...

Lately, the days fade almost before they're over
like pictures from a half-remembered dream—two friends
framed in a doorway, a sentence, a hand on a knob—

the gaps, so far, too small for anyone else to notice.
I stay quite busy at my worktable,
replacing the ruined parts of the microworld,

my fingers certain and swift inside of the machines,
inside the memorable routines of reconstruction.

Teenage Roommate

Beautiful girl, I envy you nothing, not the sleek
caramel reach of your lean arm or the lively
music of your Portuguese Skyping,
not the handsome boy a world away
who watches you cook in my kitchen
or the wealthy parents who gave you this trip.

Once, I would have killed for hair like yours,
midnight-black, straight to the hipbone in wisps.
For your tiny hands and size two denim.
I would have hated that your grandmother
was born just a year before me. But now,
I see that years are not created equal
and *which* is more important than *how many*.

Now and then you look at me with a soft face like
living alone in her fifties, what a shame.

Sometimes it feels that way, sometimes it doesn't.
I try to imagine your life at fifty, and no face comes.
No people. Nothing but rust and smoking holes,
stopped machinery, tarpits. Like a bad sci-fi movie.
I'd like to believe everyday life will continue—
solutions found, the planet healed, wars ending
in peace or at least stalemate. I'd like to believe
the Gulf can be cleaned, the pandemic won't come,
no crazy dictator will go for the red button.
I'd like to. But I don't. And I could go on.

I learned—younger than you—always to expect the worst.
In my family, not worrying meant not caring. If someone
showed up late for Sunday dinner, my mother or her mother
already had a list of hospitals to call. I thought this normal.
Maybe that's why I can't picture you at my age, Amália.

When I was 18, like you, condoms were just contraceptives.
Drugstores kept them out of sight, behind the counter:
you had to ask for them by whispered name, hoping
the pharmacist didn't know your parents, your head
bowed the way you bowed it at confession.
Boys bought them, trembling; girls just didn't.

That was before the virus. Before "safe sex"—
how strange that pair of words first seemed!
Our funeral epidemic was over by the time you were born.
There are new strains going around now,
a supervirus. Like staph.

This is not what I meant to tell you.
AIDS—super or not—isn't the end of the world.
It's just another needle in a haystack
so full of needles there's no safe place to sit
so we ride the wagon standing.

You and Artur plan to marry after college,
babies five years later. Already, you remember
a world your kids will never see. Bees.
Penguins. The North Pole. Fish dinners.

Fish dinners? You're too polite to say
"Oh, come ON. My kids will have paella!"
but too smart not to wonder whether
the world could really change that much.

It might not. But it could.
My memories tell you so.

About the Author

Jackie Sheeler is a lifelong New Yorker and a lifelong juggler: poet, performance artist, songwriter, wordrocker, publisher, blogger, producer and webmaster.

Earthquake Came to Harlem is Jackie's fourth book. Her first full-length collection, *The Memory Factory*, won the Magellan Prize and was published by Buttonwood Press in 2002. A year later she edited an anthology, *Off the Cuffs: Poetry By and About the Police* that was published by Soft Skull. In 2005, a 14-track wordrock CD, *Talk Engine*, was released to great reviews and received a substantial amount of college radio airplay. More recently, a chapbook of prose poems entitled *to[o] long* was published by Three Rooms Press.

In addition to *New York Quarterly*, her work has been widely anthologized and has appeared in *Painted Bride Quarterly*, *Phoebe*, *Slant*, and many other journals. She had the honor of writing the debut First Person essay for New York Press, and received *The Bohemian Chronicle* award for Best Short Story of 1993. Performance highlights include The People's Poetry Gathering at Cooper Union, Symphony Space, WBAI and NPR radio, CBGB's, The Poetry Project, Bowery Poetry Club and Nuyorican Poets Café (to name just a few).

Jackie has taught workshops at The Writer's Voice as well as at drug rehabs and prisons (which led to her holding for a time the title "Poet Laureate of Riker's Island", about which Martín Espada said, "Being Poet Laureate of Riker's Island is far more honorable and valuable than being Poet Laureate of the United States"). She founded the poetz.com website in 1999 which, in addition to being one of the first online literary zines, remains THE poetry event hub for NYC. 1999 also marked the beginning of her weekly reading series, The Pony, which has featured many poets of national reputation and continues to this day.

Jackie has no MFA nor any desire to obtain one; she's done fine with her GED so far and feels no need for an educational upgrade. A strong believer in workshopping, she has studied with Ellen Bass, Marie Howe, Patricia Smith, Hettie Jones, Angelo Verga and Rita Gabis, all writers she greatly admires.

About NYQ Books™

NYQ Books™ was established in 2009 as an imprint of The New York Quarterly Foundation, Inc. Its mission is to augment the *New York Quarterly* poetry magazine by providing an additional venue for poets already published in the magazine. A lifelong dream of NYQ's founding editor, William Packard, NYQ Books™ has been made possible by both growing foundation support and new technology that was not available during William Packard's lifetime. We are proud to present these books to you and hope that you will continue to support The New York Quarterly Foundation, Inc. and our poets and that you will enjoy these other titles from NYQ Books™:

Joanna Crispi	*Soldier in the Grass*
Ted Jonathan	*Bones and Jokes*
Amanda J. Bradley	*Hints and Allegations*
Ira Joe Fisher	*Songs from an Earlier Century*
Kevin Pilkington	*In the Eyes of a Dog*
Grace Zabriskie	*Poems*

Please visit our website for these and other titles:

www.nyqbooks.org

9 781935 520344